Copyright
© 2025 Shelly Zimbelman
Copyright registration pending
All rights reserved.
No part of this publication may be reproduced, stored in a retrieval system, or transmitted in any form or by any means—electronic, mechanical, photocopying, recording, or otherwise—without the prior written permission of the publisher, except in the case of brief quotations used in critical articles or reviews.

This book is based on the author's personal experiences and original reflections. Some themes are inspired by widely accepted grief and spiritual healing practices, but all content—including tables, exercises, and narratives—was uniquely created for this work. Any similarity to other published works is purely coincidental or derived from shared, publicly understood concepts within the field of grief support.

First Edition
ISBN: 979-8-9987454-4-7
Printed in the United States of America
Published by:
Legacy Light Studio, LL
St. Louis, MO
legacylightstudio.com

Cover design and interior layout by: Shelly Zimbelman
For permissions, speaking engagements, or group licensing inquiries, please contact: shelly@legacylightstudio.com

TABLE OF CONTENTS

ABOUT THE AUTHOR
INTRODUCTION
- WHAT YOU WILL GAIN FROM THIS BOOK

CHAPTER 1 – EMBRACING CHANGE
CHAPTER 2 – STRENGTH & PERSEVERANCE
CHAPTER 3 – SELF-BELIEF & CONFIDENCE
CHAPTER 4 – SUCCESS & PURPOSE
CHAPTER 5 – OVERCOMING FEAR
CHAPTER 6 – GRATITUDE & POSITIVITY
CHAPTER 7 – COURAGE & TAKING RISKS
CHAPTER 8 – MINDSET & FOCUS
CHAPTER 9 – PASSION & CREATIVITY
CHAPTER 10 – LOVE & CONNECTION
A LETTER TO THE READER
ACKNOWLEDGMENTS

About The Author

Every step forward, no matter how small, is proof of your strength and determination. Keep going — your journey is worth it.

Contact Details: shelly@legacylightstudio.com
legacylightstudio.com
hello@legacylightstudio.com

Shelly Zimbelman is a passionate writer and advocate for personal growth and resilience. Through her own experiences of overcoming challenges, she has developed a deep belief in the power of positivity and determination. With a heart for inspiring others, Shelly shares motivational words to uplift and empower readers on their journeys. Rise & Thrive is a reflection of her commitment to helping others embrace their inner strength, face adversity with courage, and celebrate the beauty of self-discovery. When not writing, Shelly enjoys painting, drawing, spending time with family, and always seeking new ways to grow and inspire.

Introduction

Life is a journey filled with challenges, triumphs, and moments of self-discovery. The key to success and happiness lies in the mindset we cultivate along the way. In this book, I share original motivational quotes to inspire you to rise above obstacles, embrace growth, and thrive in every aspect of your life. Let these words ignite your passion, fuel your determination, and remind you of the power you hold within.

INSPIRATIONAL QUOTES   LEGACYLIGHTSTUDIO.COM

What You Will Gain from This Book

Rise and Thrive offers a collection of thought-provoking quotes that will inspire, motivate, and guide you through life's journey. Each page is carefully curated to help you:

- Embrace change with an open heart and the strength to transform.
- Find strength and perseverance in the face of challenges.
- Build your self-belief and confidence to trust yourself and your abilities.
- Discover the purpose and success that comes from aligning with your true self.
- Overcome fear and step into the unknown with courage.
- Cultivate gratitude and positivity to shift your perspective and create joy.
- Take courageous risks and develop the mindset and focus needed to thrive.
- Rekindle your passion and creativity for a more fulfilled life.
- Deepen your connections with others through love and understanding.

Each quote in Rise and Thrive is a powerful reminder that the key to overcoming obstacles and living a life of purpose is within you. By reflecting on these words, you'll gain the wisdom to rise above challenges and embrace a life of growth, joy, and resilience.

Chapter 1

Embracing Change

Change is the one constant in life, yet it often feels the most unsettling. Whether expected or sudden, change challenges us to grow, adapt, and step into new versions of ourselves. It is not something to fear but rather an opportunity to evolve. In this chapter, you'll find words of encouragement to help you embrace transformation with confidence and an open heart. Let go of the past, welcome the unknown, and trust that every change leads to new possibilities.

"Every ending is a doorway to a new beginning— walk through it with courage."

INSPIRATIONAL QUOTES

LEGACYLIGHTSTUDIO.COM

"Growth begins where comfort ends—embrace the discomfort of change."

INSPIRATIONAL QUOTES LEGACYLIGHTSTUDIO.COM

"The wind may shift your path, but it can never steal your purpose."

"You are not stuck; you are simply preparing for your next breakthrough."

INSPIRATIONAL QUOTES — LEGACYLIGHTSTUDIO.COM

"Reinvention is not a sign of failure; it is proof of resilience."

INSPIRATIONAL QUOTES　　　　　　　　LEGACYLIGHTSTUDIO.COM

Chapter 2

Strength & Perseverance

Life often tests our strength in ways we never expect. True resilience is not about avoiding hardship but about rising each time we fall. Challenges shape us, teaching us to push forward even when the path seems uncertain. In this chapter, you'll find words of encouragement to remind you that perseverance is the key to success. No matter how difficult the journey, your strength will carry you through.

"Strength is not about never falling; it's about always rising."

INSPIRATIONAL QUOTES   LEGACYLIGHTSTUDIO.COM

"The road to success is paved with lessons, not limitations."

INSPIRATIONAL QUOTES LEGACYLIGHTSTUDIO.COM

"You are capable of far more than you've dared to imagine."

INSPIRATIONAL QUOTES

LEGACYLIGHTSTUDIO.COM

"Doubt may whisper, but let your determination roar."

INSPIRATIONAL QUOTES　　　　　　　　　　LEGACYLIGHTSTUDIO.COM

"Turn your struggles into stepping stones and your setbacks into comebacks."

INSPIRATIONAL QUOTES   LEGACYLIGHTSTUDIO.COM

Chapter 3

Self-Belief & Confidence

Life often tests our strength in ways we never expect. True resilience is not about avoiding hardship but about rising each time we fall. Challenges shape us, teaching us to push forward even when the path seems uncertain. In this chapter, you'll find words of encouragement to remind you that perseverance is the key to success. No matter how difficult the journey, your strength will carry you through.

"The moment you believe in yourself, the world begins to believe in you."

INSPIRATIONAL QUOTES　　　　　　　　LEGACYLIGHTSTUDIO.COM

"Confidence isn't about knowing you'll win—it's about knowing you can handle whatever comes."

INSPIRATIONAL QUOTES   LEGACYLIGHTSTUDIO.COM

"Your voice, your dreams, your light—they all matter. Never dim them for anyone."

"Fear is a liar— your potential is limitless."

INSPIRATIONAL QUOTES   LEGACYLIGHTSTUDIO.COM

"You already hold the power to create the life you desire— unlock it."

INSPIRATIONAL QUOTES LEGACYLIGHTSTUDIO.COM

Chapter 4

Success & Purpose

Success is more than just reaching a destination—it is about finding fulfillment in the journey. True success is not defined by wealth or status, but by the impact we make and the purpose we pursue. In this chapter, you'll discover insights to help you align your actions with your greater purpose, push beyond limitations, and create a life of meaning. When you chase purpose, success naturally follows.

"Success is not measured by how fast you get there, but by how deeply you grow along the way."

INSPIRATIONAL QUOTES   LEGACYLIGHTSTUDIO.COM

"Purpose is not something you find; it's something you create through action."

INSPIRATIONAL QUOTES — LEGACYLIGHTSTUDIO.COM

"Chase impact, not perfection—greatness follows those who dare to begin."

INSPIRATIONAL QUOTES LEGACYLIGHTSTUDIO.COM

"Your dreams are waiting for you to believe in them as much as they believe in you."

INSPIRATIONAL QUOTES   LEGACYLIGHTSTUDIO.COM

"A fulfilled life is not built in a day, but in the moments we choose to keep going."

INSPIRATIONAL QUOTES   LEGACYLIGHTSTUDIO.COM

Chapter 5

Overcoming Fear

Fear is a powerful force that can hold us back from reaching our true potential. It whispers doubts, builds walls, and keeps us in our comfort zones. But the truth is, fear only has as much power as we give it. In this chapter, you'll find inspiration to face your fears head-on, step beyond hesitation, and embrace the courage within you. Growth lies on the other side of fear—dare to push forward.

"Fear is nothing more than a shadow—walk through it, and you'll find the light."

"Your dreams should scare you a little; that's how you know they're worth chasing."

INSPIRATIONAL QUOTES — LEGACYLIGHTSTUDIO.COM

"Fear is the greatest thief of opportunity—don't let it steal your future."

INSPIRATIONAL QUOTES — LEGACYLIGHTSTUDIO.COM

"Courage isn't the absence of fear; it's taking action despite it."

INSPIRATIONAL QUOTES LEGACYLIGHTSTUDIO.COM

"Step outside of fear, and you step into your true potential."

INSPIRATIONAL QUOTES   LEGACYLIGHTSTUDIO.COM

Chapter 6

Gratitude & Positivity

Gratitude is a powerful shift in perspective—it turns what we have into enough and opens the door for more joy in our lives. Positivity isn't about ignoring hardships; it's about choosing to focus on the good even in difficult times. In this chapter, you'll find inspiration to cultivate gratitude, embrace optimism, and create a mindset that attracts abundance and happiness. The more you appreciate, the more life gives you to be grateful for.

"A grateful heart attracts abundance in all forms."

INSPIRATIONAL QUOTES	LEGACYLIGHTSTUDIO.COM

"Happiness is not something you chase—it's something you create through gratitude."

"Even in the darkest moments, there is something to be thankful for."

INSPIRATIONAL QUOTES　　　　　　　　LEGACYLIGHTSTUDIO.COM

"The more you focus on the good, the more good you will see."

INSPIRATIONAL QUOTES   LEGACYLIGHTSTUDIO.COM

"Gratitude is the bridge between what you have and what you desire."

INSPIRATIONAL QUOTES

LEGACYLIGHTSTUDIO.COM

Chapter 7

Courage & Taking Risks

Courage is not the absence of fear but the decision to move forward despite it. Taking risks is what leads to growth, discovery, and success. Every great achievement begins with a moment of bravery—choosing to step outside your comfort zone and trust yourself. In this chapter, you'll find motivation to embrace uncertainty, take bold action, and unlock the limitless potential that lies beyond fear. The biggest risk is never taking one at all.

"Nothing great ever came from a place of comfort."

"Dare to take the leap—the net will appear."

INSPIRATIONAL QUOTES LEGACYLIGHTSTUDIO.COM

"The biggest risk is not taking one at all."

"Your future self is waiting on you to be bold today."

INSPIRATIONAL QUOTES   LEGACYLIGHTSTUDIO.COM

"Every great success story begins with a moment of courage."

INSPIRATIONAL QUOTES　　　　　　　　LEGACYLIGHTSTUDIO.COM

Chapter 8

Mindset & Focus

Your mindset shapes your reality, and where you direct your focus determines your path. A strong, positive mindset helps you navigate challenges, stay disciplined, and push through obstacles. In this chapter, you'll find encouragement to cultivate mental clarity, strengthen your focus, and align your thoughts with your goals. When you master your mindset, you unlock the power to create the life you desire.

"Your mindset determines your reality—choose wisely."

INSPIRATIONAL QUOTES　　　　　　　　LEGACYLIGHTSTUDIO.COM

"Focus on progress, not perfection."

INSPIRATIONAL QUOTES LEGACYLIGHTSTUDIO.COM

"What you focus on expands—direct your energy toward growth."

INSPIRATIONAL QUOTES　　　　　　　　LEGACYLIGHTSTUDIO.COM

"Your thoughts shape your world—guard them carefully."

INSPIRATIONAL QUOTES

LEGACYLIGHTSTUDIO.COM

"Clarity of mind leads to clarity of action."

Chapter 9

Passion & Creativity

Life often tests our strength in ways we never expect. True resilience is not about avoiding hardship but about rising each time we fall. Challenges shape us, teaching us to push forward even when the path seems uncertain. In this chapter, you'll find words of encouragement to remind you that perseverance is the key to success. No matter how difficult the journey, your strength will carry you through.

"Passion is the fuel that ignites purpose."

"The world needs your unique voice—don't be afraid to share it."

INSPIRATIONAL QUOTES　　　　　　　　　　LEGACYLIGHTSTUDIO.COM

"Creativity is intelligence having fun—let your imagination run wild."

INSPIRATIONAL QUOTES   LEGACYLIGHTSTUDIO.COM

"Find what sets your soul on fire and pursue it relentlessly."

INSPIRATIONAL QUOTES

LEGACYLIGHTSTUDIO.COM

"Innovation is born from those who dare to think differently."

INSPIRATIONAL QUOTES   LEGACYLIGHTSTUDIO.COM

Chapter 10

Love & Connection

Love is the foundation of a meaningful life. It is what binds us together, fuels our compassion, and gives us purpose. True connection comes when we open our hearts—to ourselves, to others, and to the world around us. In this chapter, you'll find inspiration to embrace love in all its forms, nurture deep connections, and lead with kindness. The more love you give, the more it multiplies.

"Love is the most powerful force in the universe— lead with it always."

INSPIRATIONAL QUOTES   LEGACYLIGHTSTUDIO.COM

"True connection begins when we allow ourselves to be seen."

INSPIRATIONAL QUOTES LEGACYLIGHTSTUDIO.COM

The energy you put into the world is the energy that will return to you."

INSPIRATIONAL QUOTES LEGACYLIGHTSTUDIO.COM

"Kindness costs nothing but means everything."

INSPIRATIONAL QUOTES   LEGACYLIGHTSTUDIO.COM

"At the heart of every great life is love—love for yourself, love for others, and love for the journey."

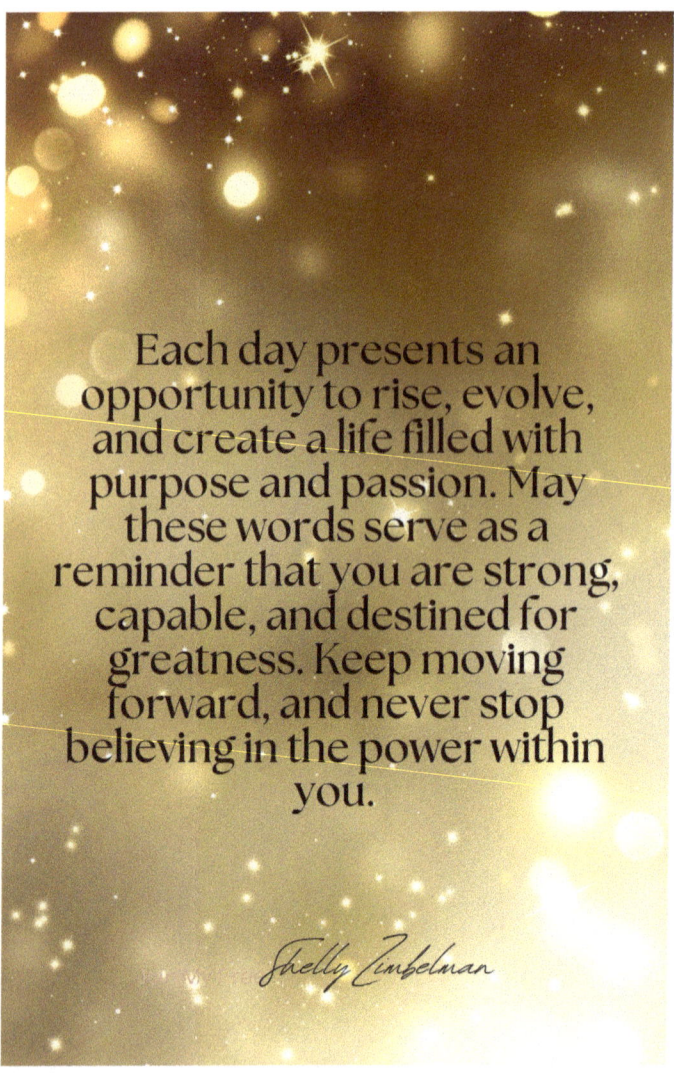

ACKNOWLEDGMENTS

I WOULD LIKE TO EXPRESS MY DEEPEST GRATITUDE TO THE FOLLOWING INDIVIDUALS FOR THEIR UNWAVERING SUPPORT AND GUIDANCE THROUGHOUT THE CREATION OF THIS BOOK:

TO MY FAMILY AND FRIENDS, WHOSE LOVE AND ENCOURAGEMENT HAVE BEEN A CONSTANT SOURCE OF STRENGTH.

TO THE MENTORS AND SPIRITUAL GUIDES WHO HAVE HELPED ME DEEPEN MY UNDERSTANDING OF HEALING, SPIRITUALITY, AND SELF-EMPOWERMENT.

TO THE READERS WHO HAVE INSPIRED ME WITH THEIR COURAGE AND RESILIENCE, AND WHO CONTINUE TO LIGHT THE PATH FOR OTHERS.

AND TO THOSE WHO HAVE WALKED THIS JOURNEY WITH ME, BOTH IN SPIRIT AND IN PERSON. YOUR PRESENCE IN MY LIFE HAS MADE ALL THE DIFFERENCE.

INSPIRATIONAL QUOTES   LEGACYLIGHTSTUDIO.COM

www.ingramcontent.com/pod-product-compliance
Lightning Source LLC
Chambersburg PA
CBHW040322050426
42453CB00017B/2437